THE BEST OF
ARETHA FRANKLIN

WISE PUBLICATIONS
London/New York/Paris/Sydney/Copenhagen/Madrid

Exclusive Distributors:
Music Sales Limited
14-15 Berners Street,
London W1T 3LJ, UK.
Music Sales Pty Limited
20 Resolution Drive,
Caringbah, NSW 2229,
Australia.

Order No.AM959563
ISBN 0-7119-7478-0
This book © Copyright 1991, 1999 by Wise Publications

Unauthorised reproduction of any part of this publication by any means including photocopying is an infringement of copyright.

Cover design by Chloë Alexander
Photographs courtesy of London Features International

Printed in Great Britain

Your Guarantee of Quality
As publishers, we strive to produce every book to the highest commercial standards. The book has been carefully designed to minimise awkward page turns and to make playing from it a real pleasure. Particular care has been given to specifying acid-free, neutral-sized paper made from pulps which have not been elemental chlorine bleached. This pulp is from farmed sustainable forests and was produced with special regard for the environment. Throughout, the printing and binding have been planned to ensure a sturdy, attractive publication which should give years of enjoyment. If your copy fails to meet our high standards, please inform us and we will gladly replace it.

Bridge Over Troubled Water 14
I Knew You Were Waiting (For Me) 46
I Say A Little Prayer 24
Jumpin' Jack Flash 28
Let It Be 19
Respect 4
Sisters Are Doin' It For Themselves 38
Spanish Harlem 7
Try A Little Tenderness 42
Walk On By 36
(You Make Me Feel Like) A Natural Woman 10

Respect

WORDS & MUSIC BY OTIS REDDING

© Copyright 1965 East/Memphis Music Corporation & Time Music.
Assigned to Irving Music Incorporated 1982.
Warner Chappell Music Limited, 129 Park Street, London W1.
All Rights Reserved.
International Copyright Secured.

Spanish Harlem

WORDS & MUSIC BY JERRY LEIBER & PHIL SPECTOR

© Copyright 1960 Progressive Music Publishing Company
Incorporated & Trio Music Company Incorporated, U.S.A.
Carlin Music Corporation, Iron Bridge House, 3 Bridge Approach, London NW1 for the UK, Eire,
Israel, the British Dominions, Colonies, Overseas Territories and Dependencies
(excluding Canada, Australia and New Zealand).
All Rights Reserved.
International Copyright Secured.

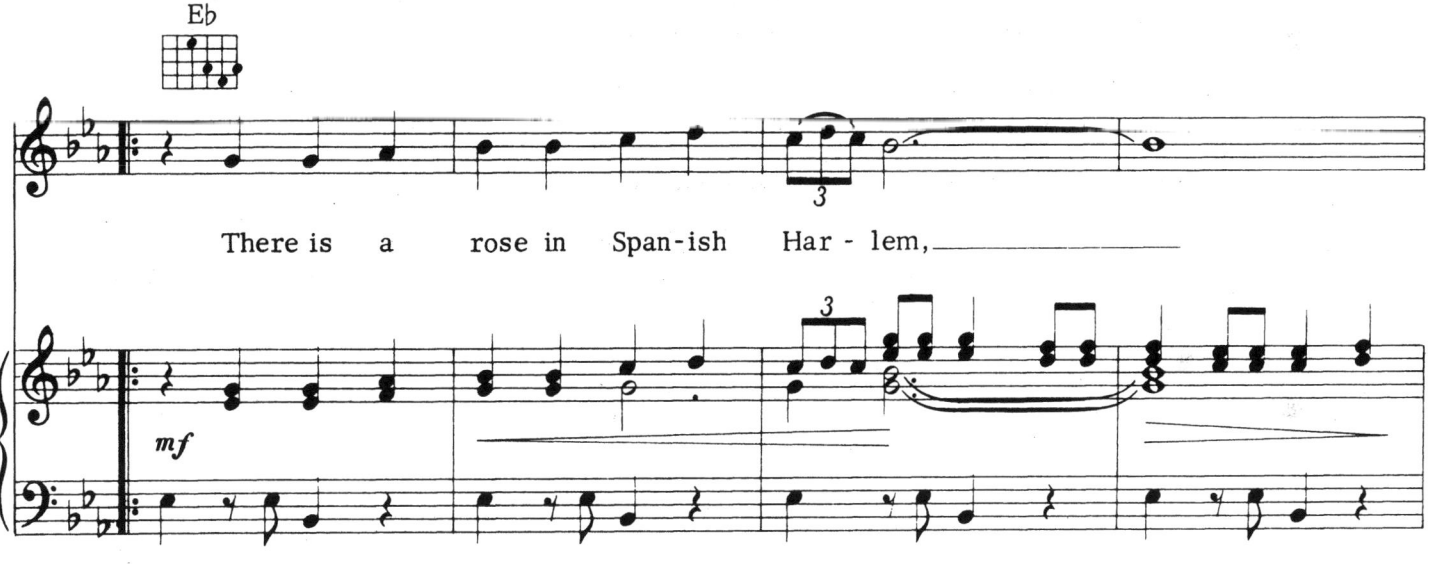

There is a rose in Span-ish Har-lem,

A rare rose up in Span-ish Har-lem,

7

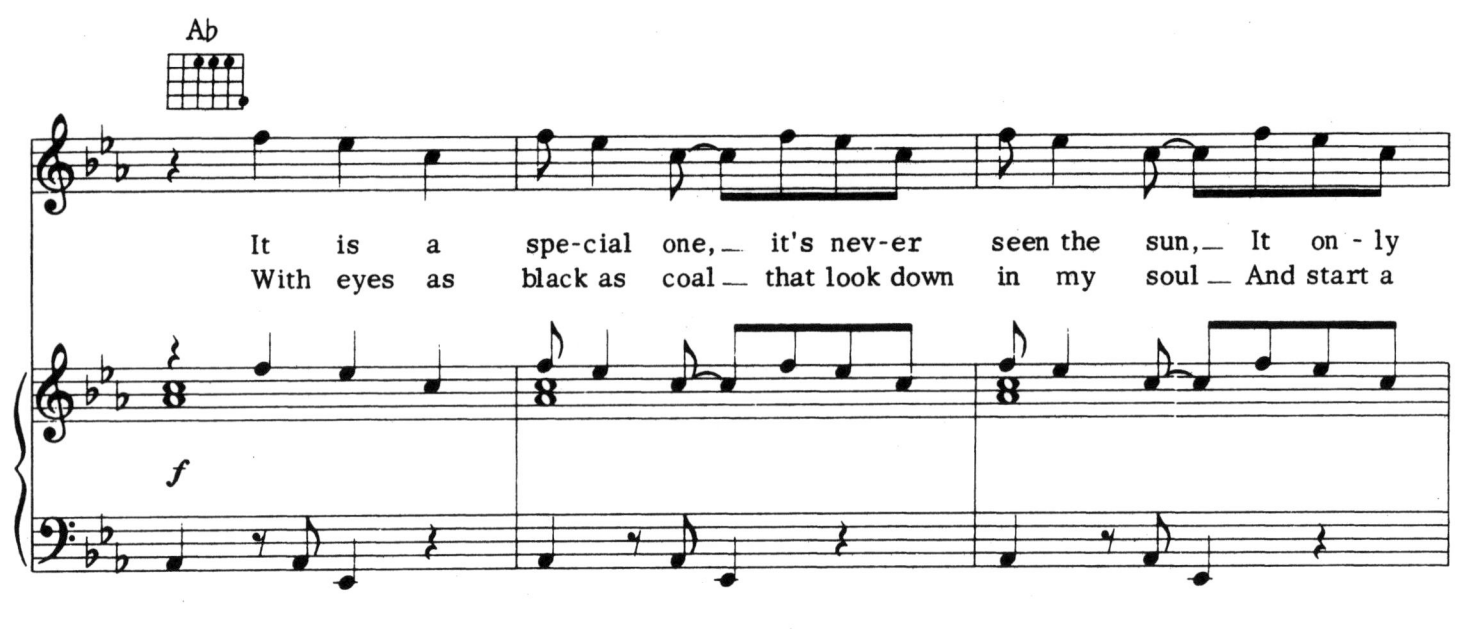
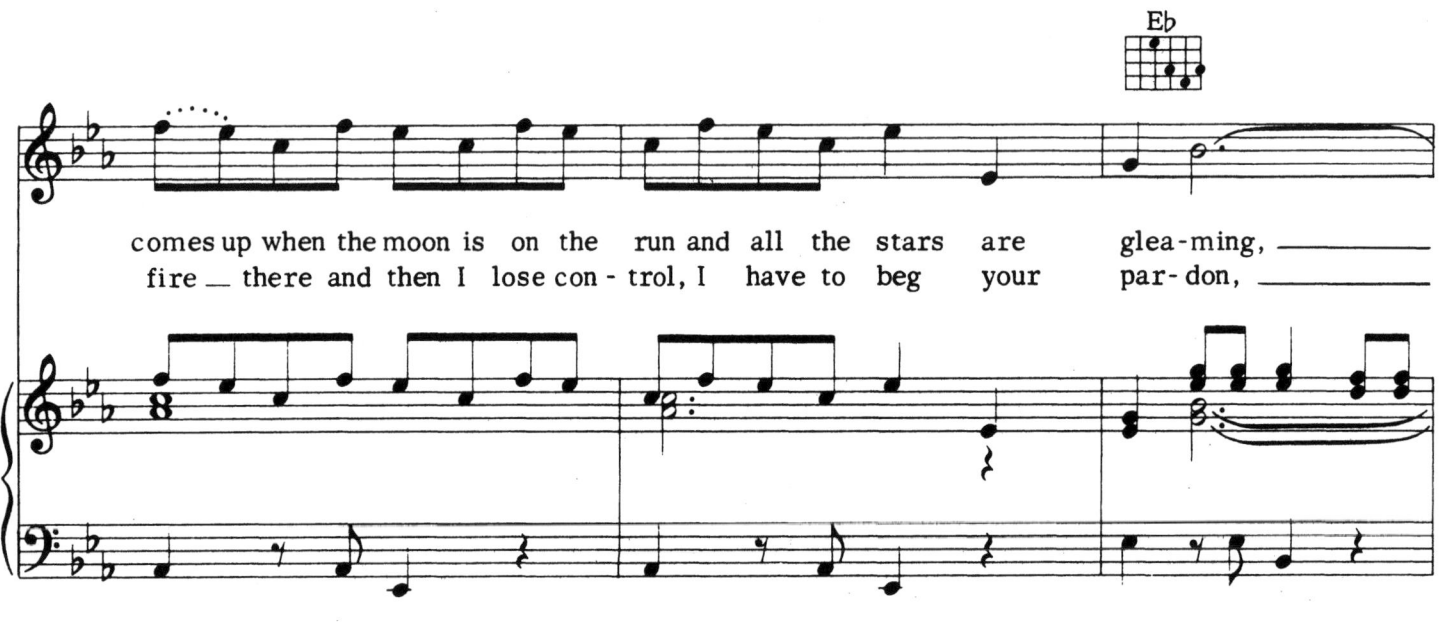
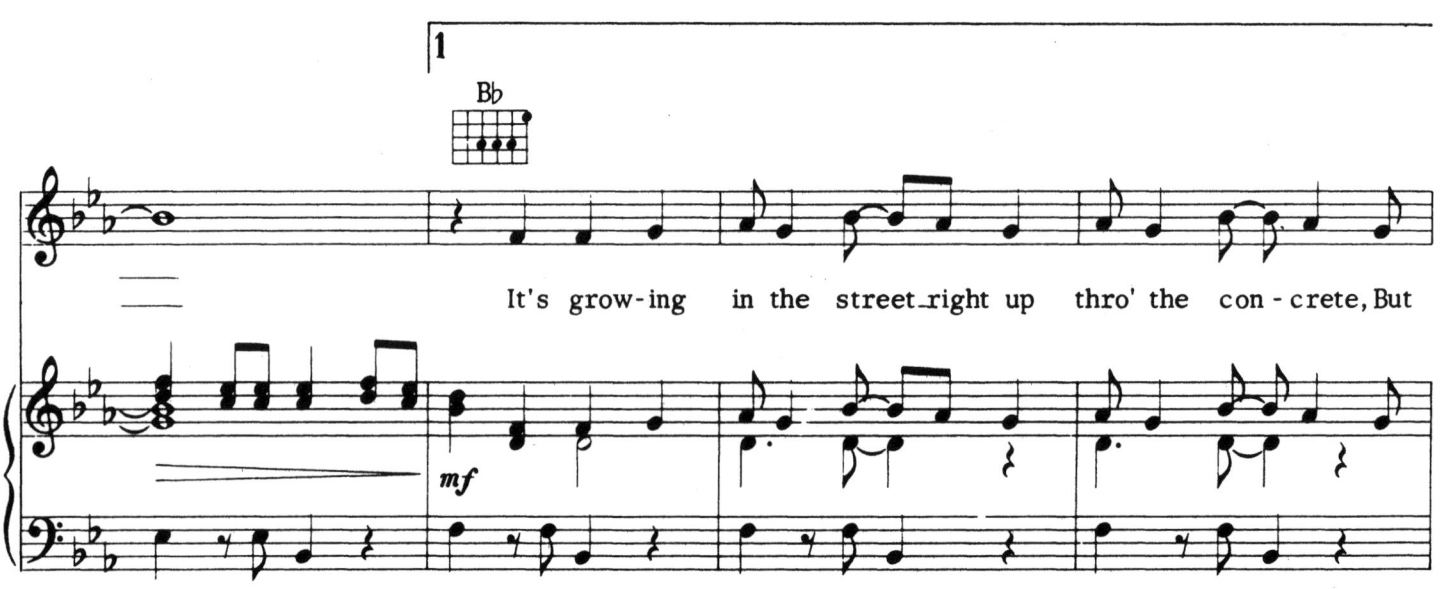

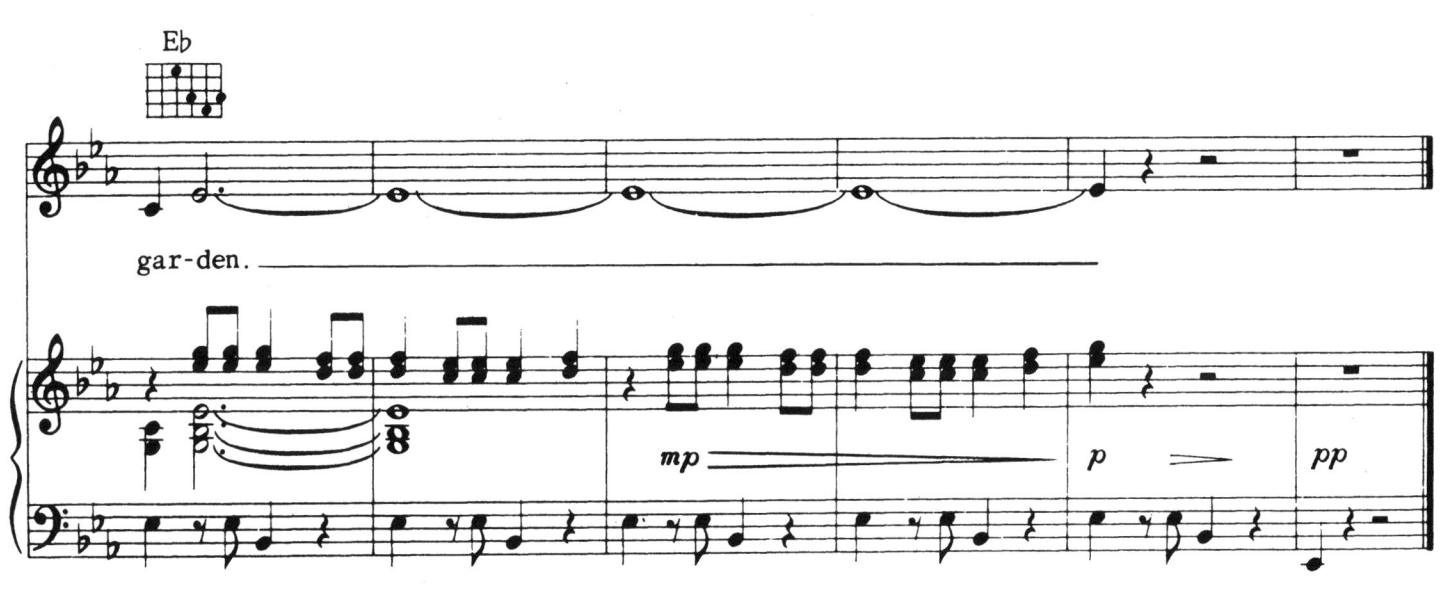

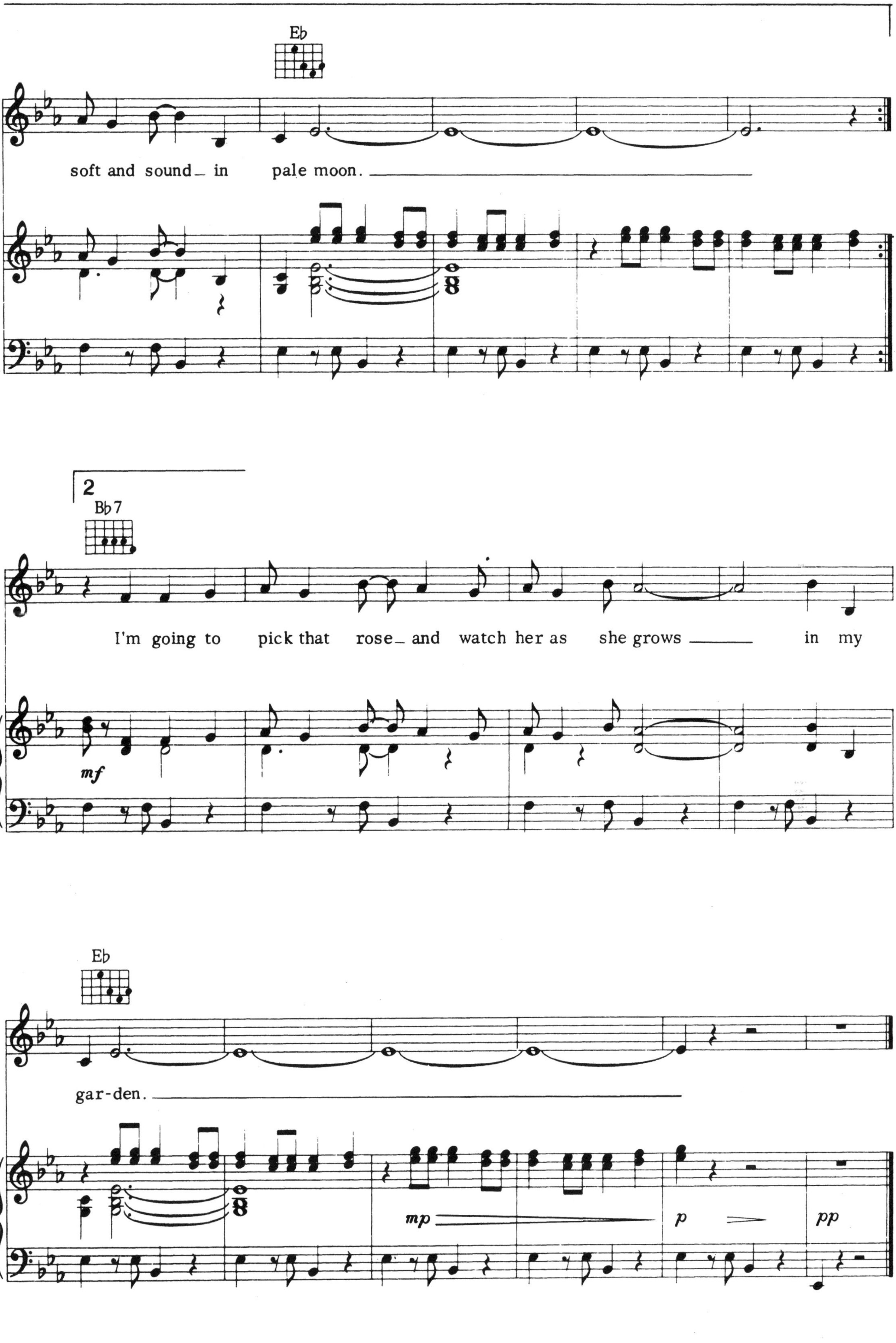

E♭
soft and sound_ in pale moon.
2
B♭7
I'm going to pick that rose_ and watch her as she grows in my
mf
E♭
gar-den.
mp
p
pp

Let It Be

WORDS & MUSIC BY JOHN LENNON & PAUL McCARTNEY

© Copyright 1970 Northern Songs, under licence to EMI Songs Limited,
127 Charing Cross Road, London WC2.
All Rights Reserved.
International Copyright Secured.

Slowly

When I find myself in times of trouble Mother Mary comes to me Speaking words of wisdom, Let it be and in my hour of darkness She is

I Say A Little Prayer

WORDS BY HAL DAVID. MUSIC BY BURT BACHARACH

© Copyright 1966 Blue Seas Music Incorporated & Jac Music Company Incorporated, USA.
MCA Music Limited, 77 Fulham Palace Road, London SW6.
All Rights Reserved.
International Copyright Secured.

Jumpin' Jack Flash

WORDS & MUSIC BY MICK JAGGER & KEITH RICHARDS

© Copyright 1968 ABKCO Music Incorporated, U.S.A.
Westminster Music Limited, Suite 2.07, Plaza 535 Kings Road, London SW10.
All Rights Reserved.
International Copyright Secured.

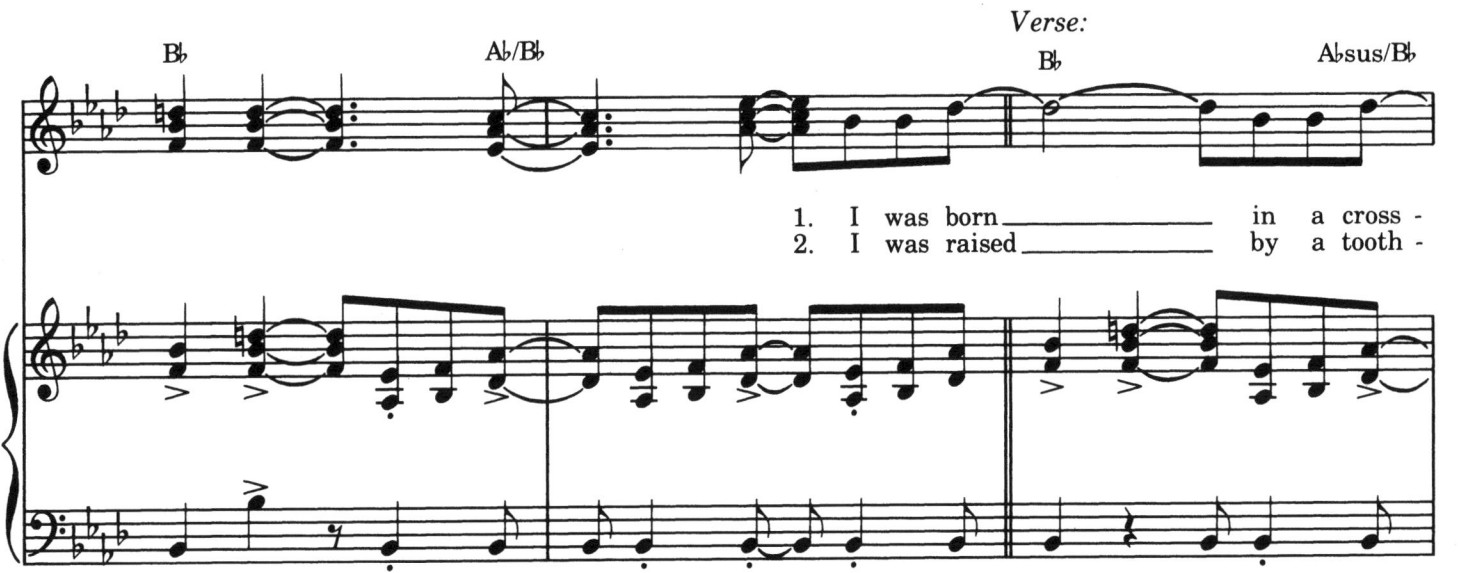
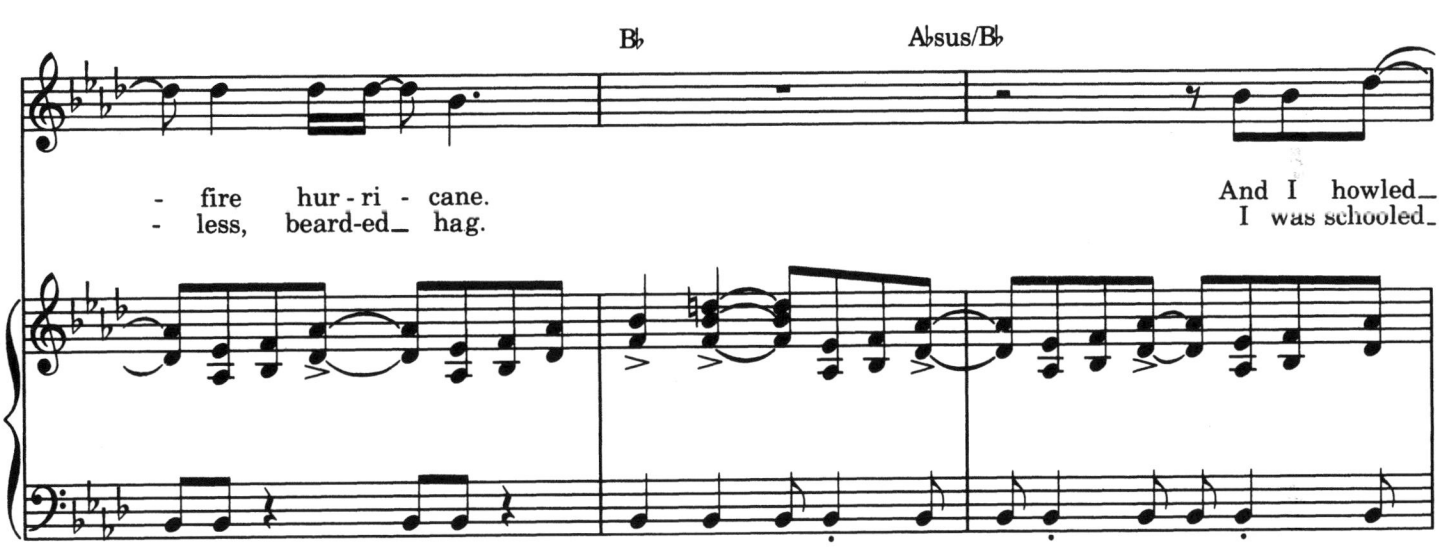
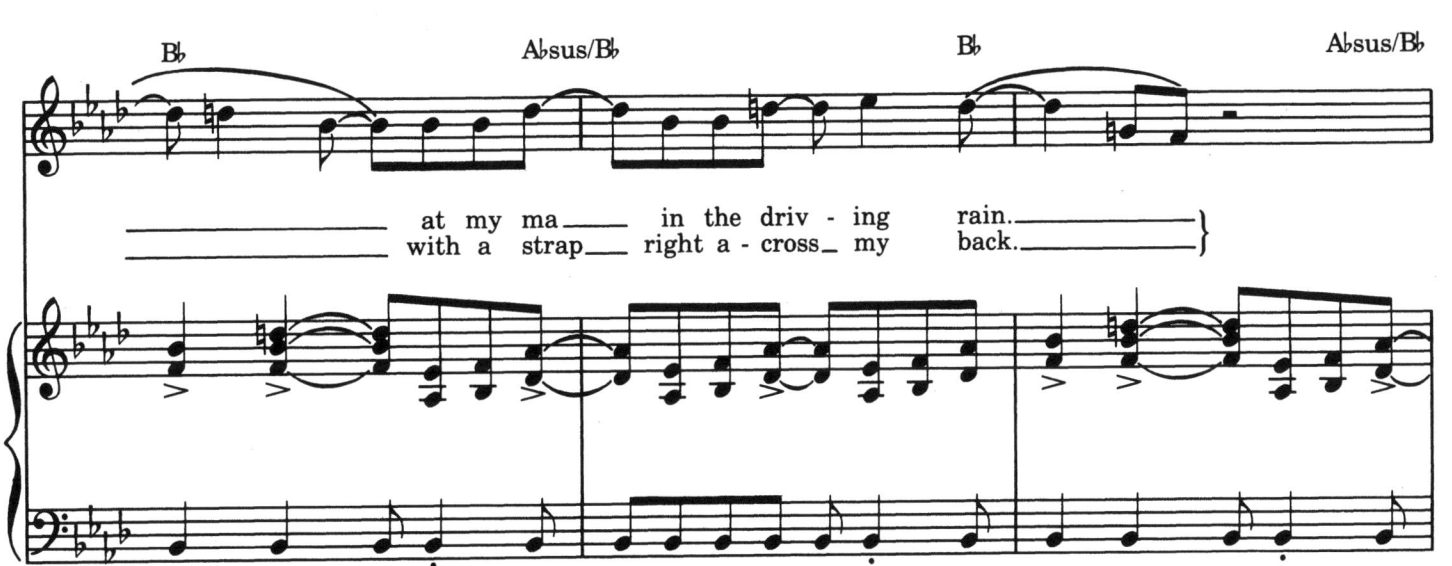

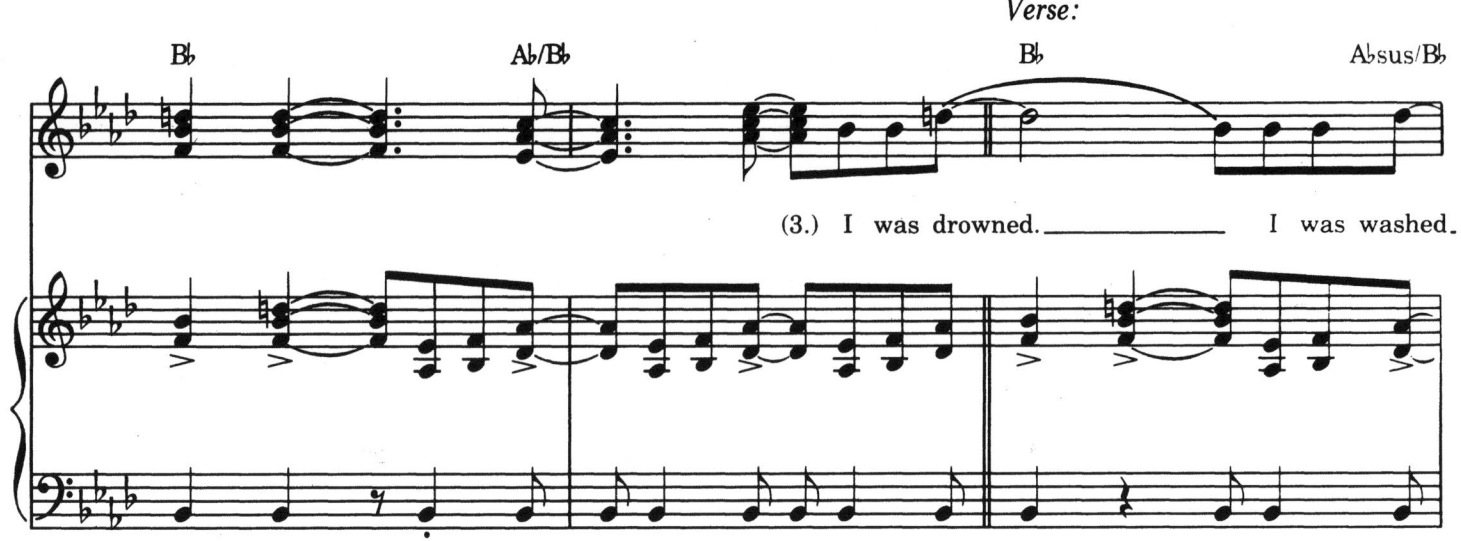
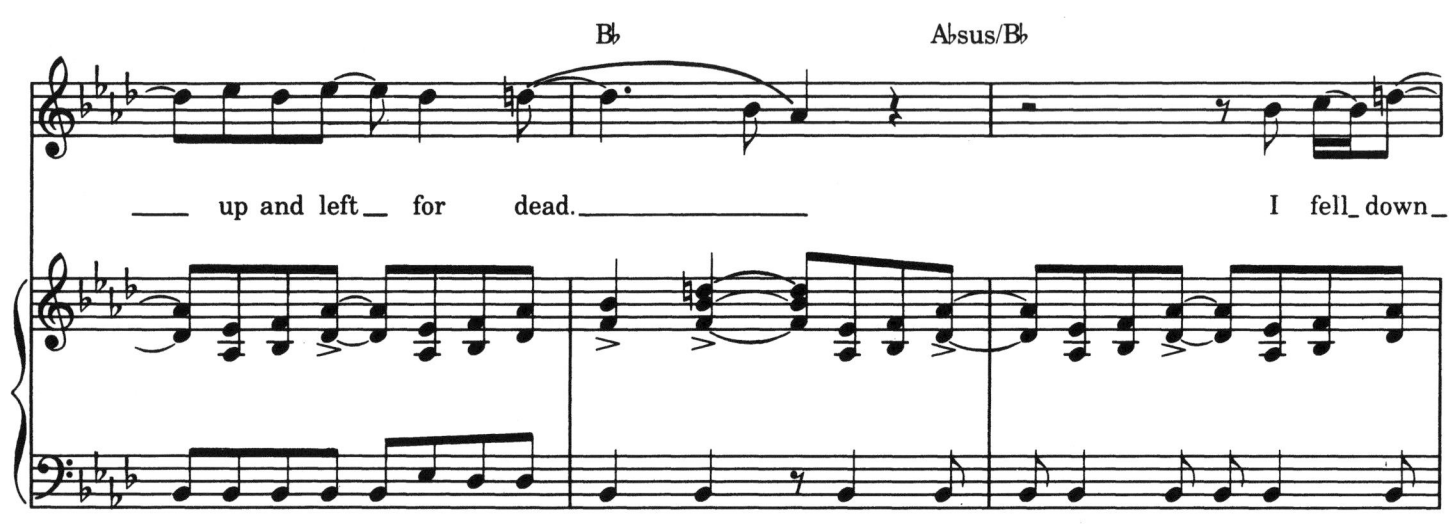
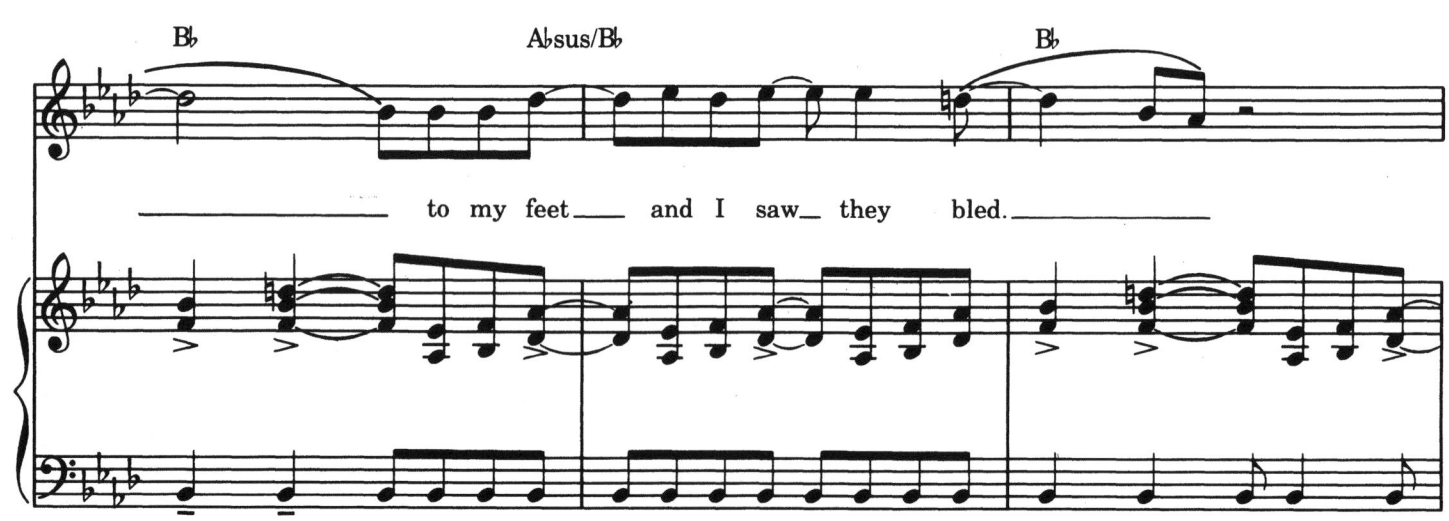

pri-vate, 'Cause each time I see you, I break down and cry.
tears and the sad-ness you gave me when you said good-bye.

Walk on by,___ Don't stop, Walk on by.___

___ Don't stop, Walk on by.___

Sisters Are Doing It For Themselves

WORDS & MUSIC BY A. LENNOX & D. A. STEWART

© Copyright 1985 D'N'A Limited/BMG Music Publishing Limited.
All rights administered by BMG Music Publishing Limited,
Bedford House, 69-79 Fulham High Street, London SW6 3JW.
All Rights Reserved.
International Copyright Secured.

Now, there was a time when they used to say that be-hind ev-'ry "great man" there had to be a "great wom-an." But oh, in these times of change you know that it's no long-er true. So we're com-in' out of the kitch-

-en 'cause there's some-thing we for-got to say to you. We say:

Sis-ters are do-in' it for them-selves, stand-in' on their own two feet and ring-in' on their own bells. Sis-ters are do-in' it for them-selves. Now, this is a song to cel-e-brate the con-scious lib-er-a-tion of the fe--male state. Moth-ers, daugh-ters, and their daugh-ters, too, yeah, wom-an to wom-an, we're sing-ing with you. The "in-fe-ri-or sex" has got a new ex--te-ri-or. We got doc-tors, law-yers, pol--i-ti-cians, too. Ev-

40

-'ry-bod-y ___ take __ a look a-round. ___

Can you see, can you see, can you see, there's a wom-an right next to you. ___

D.S. 𝄋 al Coda ⊕
We say:

Coda ⊕
Now we ain't mak-in' sto-

-ries and we ain't lay-in' plans. Don't you know that a man still loves a

D.S. 𝄋 and fade
wom-an and a wom-an still loves a man. __ (Just the same though.) __

41

Try A Little Tenderness

WORDS & MUSIC BY HARRY WOODS, JIMMY CAMPBELL & REG CONNELLY

© Copyright 1932 & 1960 for all countries Campbell Connelly & Company Limited,
8/9 Frith Street, London W1.
All Rights Reserved.
International Copyright Secured.

Slowly with expression

(Freely)

In the bus-tle of to-day ___ We're all in-clined to miss ___ Lit-tle things that mean so much, A word, a smile, a kiss, ___ When a

With a ten-der word of love ___ You can make the wrong things right, ___ Charm a-way the clouds of grey, And make this drab world bright. ___ When your

woman loves a man, _____ He's a hero in her
worries drag you down, _____ It's so easy to for-

eyes. _____ And a hero he can always be, If
get. _____ But make the effort just the same, And

he'll just realize.
see the thrill you'll get.

CHORUS *Tenderly*

She may be weary,
Women do get weary, Wearing the same shabby dress,

And when she's wea-ry, Try a lit-tle ten-der-ness.

You know she's wait-ing, Just an-ti-ci-pat-ing, Things she may nev-er poss-ess. While she's with-out them, Try a lit-tle ten-der-ness.

It's not just sen-ti-men-tal, She

has her grief and care, And a word that's soft and gen-tle, Makes it ea-si-er to bear. You won't re-gret it, Wo-men don't for-get it, Love is their whole hap-pi-ness. It's all so ea-sy Try a lit-tle ten-der-ness.

ness.

I Knew You Were Waiting (For Me)

WORDS & MUSIC BY SIMON CLIMIE & DENNIS MORGAN

© Copyright 1986 Chrysalis Music Limited for the World (50%).
© Copyright 1986 Little Shop of Morgan Songs, USA (50%).
Rights administered in the UK & Eire By Chrysalis Music Limited.
All Rights Reserved.
International Copyright Secured.

Lyrics:
(1.) Like a warrior that fights and wins the battle, I know the taste of victory. Though I went through some nights consumed by the shadows, I was crippled emotionally, mm. Somehow I made it through the

heart-ache, yes I did, ___ I es-caped. ___ I found my way out of the dark-ness, kept my faith, ___ kept my faith. ___ When the ri-ver was deep I did-n't fal-ter, when the mountain was high ___ I still be-lieved. ___ When the val-ley was low ___ it did-n't stop ___ me, no ___ no. I knew you were wait-ing, I knew you were wait-ing for me. ___ So we were drawn

VERSE 2:
With an endless desire
I kept on searching
Sure in time our eyes would meet.

And like the bridge is on fire
The hurt is over
One touch and you set me free.

I don't regret a single moment no I don't, looking back
When I think of all those disappointments, I just laugh, I just laugh.